Style

Developing Chic Taste for Style and Fashion Made Easy

By

Sofia Lundgren

information is without contract or any type of guarantee assurance.

The trademarks that are used are without any consent, and the publication of the trademark is without permission or backing by the trademark owner. All trademarks and brands within this book are for clarifying purposes only and are the owned by the owners themselves, not affiliated with this document.

Contents

Introduction

Being fashionable and looking great is something that every woman aspires to. It can also be quite intimidating, especially if you do not know where to start in regards to the items to purchase and what you should wear. Even though you have tried to use magazines to copy outfits that you thought were amazing, you may be surprised to find that they are not working for you. This only happens when you do not understand some fundamentals of fashion.

This is a book which will change the game of how you dress, and it will make the daunting subject of fashion very easy for you to comprehend. It is full of tips and tricks that will help you to develop a chic taste, so that wherever you go, people acknowledge you for having excellent style.

Being chic is all about paying close attention to what you are wearing, and how it flatters the body. It is also about ensuring you have key items in your wardrobe and are confident enough to carry yourself with head held high.

Do not worry about changing your entire wardrobe in order to achieve that chic look. This book will help you work with what you have, and let you know which essential items should be added to your wardrobe to keep it chic and classy. Follow the tips that are within this book, and before long, you will be the style example that many others are looking to emulate.

Chapter 1:
Build a Basic Outfit

Have you ever wondered how some people appear to have stepped out of the pages of a magazine every time that you see them? They look amazing, with not a hair out of place and amazing clothes on their bodies. There is an expression that you should wear the clothes, and they should not wear you. This book is about how you can achieve this, and develop your own unique and chic taste. As you prepare to delve into fashion, you need to understand the elements of a basic outfit. Here are the things that you need.

Start with a Base

Every outfit begins with a base, which is what your first layer of clothing is called. The base is typically made up of one of two elements. These could be a skirt or trousers at the bottom, with something else on the top, or you could need a dress. There are some factors that you need to consider when choosing your base, and these are as follows: -

- The activities that you are going to carry out for the day. You need to know what you will be doing as this will determine the type of clothes that you need. If you are going out for the evening, you will need something different than if you are going out to exercises.

- Next, you should consider how you want to feel in your clothes. Are you looking to feel comfortable as you get through your errands for the day, professional or confident? This will also help you select the colors and styles that you prefer.

- Keep in mind the weather you are dressing up for and the means that you will use to get from one place to another. You may need to dress in layers if the temperature is cold or wear something light and airy when it is hot. If you are walking, this will determine the type of shoes that you wear, and if you are in getting in and out of a car, you can be a little less practical.

What you choose as your base is where the definition of your style begins, as it is these elements that will stand out the most when you have finished dressing.

Build on Your Base

Once you have your first layer sorted, you can begin to build on it by adding more layers. There are instances when this is not necessary, because the weather does not require it, or your base outfit looks complete as it is. If you do want to add layers, you can choose from a shirt, jackets, blazers, scarves and so on.

There is a strategy that you should use when adding layers. Begin with the items that are as close to your body as possible, and those that are the most fitting. Your layers should become more voluminous as you go along.

When it comes to layers, you can change up your outfits by choosing items which are of varying lengths, different colors and patterns and textures.

Dressing your Feet

Once you have your base and additional layers, the shoes are the next element of your outfit. There are so many different designs and styles to choose from that you should enjoy this part of picking your outfit immensely. When selecting the colors for your shoes, you can choose a color that matches one of the parts of your base outfit, or something in an entirely contrasting color so that it stands out. The shoes that you wear can add the most important element of style to your outfit.

Pick out your Accessories

It is accessories that will give your outfit that final polish that it needs, adding the essential chic taste to your personal style. There are so many different ways that you can accessorize your outfit, including the addition of jewelry, bags, watches, hats and so on. There is a delicate balance between excellent accessorizing and taking it a step too far.

To get this balance right, ensure that you have on accessory which can stand out as a statement piece. This is the one that will draw the attention of any person who is looking at your outfit. You can then add other accessories based on how this works with your overall look.

Once you have put all these elements together, you should be able to put together a great outfit. It is essential that you think through each piece that you are putting on, ensuring that it adds some value to your complete look. Fashion gets messy when you do not take the time to think through your outfit, and instead, simply throw some items on.

Achieving the Chic Look

You do not need to rush out and purchase an entirely new wardrobe so that you can look chic in your clothing. There are several things that you can do. The first is to make sure that all your clothes are clean and steamed or pressed. This will help you immediately appear to be polished and put together, which are essential for chic style.

Your accessories can also add to your chic look. Choosing gold pieces, whether they are jewelry, bags or shoes will make you look fantastic and chic. You should aim to have one gold piece that makes a statement and draws the attention of an observer to your overall look.

When pairing or choosing your base layer, go for something that is monochrome. Neutral colors are the best for helping you look as though you dressed intentionally. Then, you can add on accessories that are subtle to compliment your total look.

Finally, do not forget to pay attention to your face. Keeping your skin clean and clear is the first step to looking chic. In addition, you cannot go wrong with well-cut hair and a bold red lip.

Now that you know how to put together the basic outfit, you need to identify your personal style so that you know how to class it up.

Chapter 2:
Identify Your Personal Style

Each and every person is different, having a different way that they view the world and participate in it. That is why when it comes to fashion and clothing, there are so many different designers creating a wide array of interesting looks. Before you can start to develop your chic style, you need to be able to identify your existing personal style. This will help you make the right decisions to spruce up your wardrobe and your total look. So how do you try to find out what you are all about? You can follow these steps: -

Find out What Inspires You

Looking at your clothing now, you will notice that there is a consistent tone and way that you prefer to address. You need to figure out what inspires you to dress as you do. This is best done by creating a list. Write down how you like to feel when you are all dressed up, and look through a fashion magazine to identify which designers are your style icons.

You may also be inspired to dress like a particular celebrity, so look at the elements within their outfits that appeal the most to you. Go through a leading fashion magazine and see what people are wearing and how the outfits look on their bodies. This is the first step to understanding what makes you feel your very best.

Think about your Lifestyle

You may find that you are inspired by great evening dresses or suits that make you feel polished and sexy. The dilemma is that you cannot wear this type of clothing all day every day, as there are places where it would not be appropriate. Therefore, when working towards identifying your personal style, you need to think about your lifestyle, and what you do each day.

This way, you can ensure that the pieces of clothing you select are a reflection of what inspires you, but, they also fit into your work life, the persona you want to portray and what you have to do on a daily basis.

Consider this, you may love an evening dress because it makes you feel sexy by hugging all the right curves and giving you an amazing silhouette. Instead of wearing a sexy dress to work, you may choose to wear a pair of dark skinny jeans that hug all your curves, and top this with a white blazer which accentuates that curve of your waist. You still look and feel great, while ensuring your style and your lifestyle are at par.

Audit your Closet

Take every item of clothing that you have out of your closet, so that you are able to sort through the items that you wear. If there are items that you have not worn for at least six months, set them aside. These are the types of items that you feel do not define your personal style, even though you have not said anything out loud. Once you have sorted out your clothes, you will be left with a smaller wardrobe that reflects who you really are.

Go through these pieces and see whether any of them say 'chic.' If they do not, you will be able to purchase some wardrobe essentials which you can use to mix and match the items that you already have. When your closet is no longer cluttered, you will be amazed by how many great clothes that you actually own. A cluttered closet makes it challenging to identify your key items.

Consider your Confidence

How great do you feel when you dress you and leave your home? Are you confident and free, or do you spend a large amount of time fiddling and adjusting your clothing so that you look alright? With a world that is obsessed with smaller clothes sizes and thin figures, it is easy for anyone to feel inadequate with their personal style.

What happens, in this case, is that you sometimes end up buying clothing that is smaller than your actual size, and you attempt to squash yourself into the clothing so that you appear slimmer. This makes it a challenge for you to stand tall and feel great in what you are wearing. Being uncomfortable will not help you feel chic.

Instead of torturing yourself in this way, make sure that you always buy clothes that fit your shape, no matter what size is written on the size tag. When your clothes are well fitting, you will feel confident and look as though you are comfortable in your own style. That is the ultimate expression of Chic.

Do not Do It Alone

When you feel lost in identifying your personal style, do not give into dismay, and instead, look for someone who is professional and experienced, and can offer you help. Go into a clothing store and explain that you want to express yourself in a certain way but remain chic as well. You should be able to find an enthusiastic shop assistant who can guide you towards excellent clothing pieces that suit you.

If you are too intimidated to go into a shop, you can choose to get advice from a professional photographer who is focused on fashion. They know how to make photos fall and fit the body well so that people always look amazing. With help from the outside, you will find a way that you can accentuate your best assets while expressing yourself with class.

Be Yourself

If you have a quirky character, and like clothing that is bright and colorful with bold prints, you may be dismayed and imagine that you cannot achieve the perfect chic. To enjoy fashion, you need to embrace yourself and ever factor that affects your style. Achieving and expressing chic taste is not about changing all your clothes, it is about how you choose to put yourself together.

You need to have a personal style that you can celebrate, which expresses your taste as an individual and also defines your personality. Therefore, when you are selecting clothes, use the guidelines that have been provided, and remember to stay true to yourself.

Chapter 3:
Developing your Personal Style

Now that you know all about how to identify your personal style, you can easily move on to the next step, which is the developing of your personal style. How you project yourself is not something that you can decide in a day, as a simple way to put together your clothing for a complete look. It is something that takes time to build, so that you experiencing experimentation before you fully learn what you want to look at.

Consider How You Spend Your Day

You have identified what your personal style is, now you need to make it as practical and comfortable as possible. This way, you will be better able to fully enjoy it. This begins with thinking about what you are doing for a living. If you are in a serious profession, such as accounting or auditing, it is unlikely that you will wear ripped jeans and a white t-shirt. If you have to be on your feet all day, then amazing high heels lost some of their appeal.

The best thing that you can do when developing your personal style is think about your job, and then ensure that you have enough clothes to be comfortable with your work. You can then choose to add on some signature accessories that allow you to have more expression.

Think About your Life Goals

As you develop your personal style, you need to look a little deeper than just what you like to wear and your favored colored palate. You need to consider what you are looking to achieve in life. For example, you may be thinking about a change in career, where you want a job that will ensure you are at the top of the leader board. Can you visualize what you should look like for this? Great.

In another scenario, you may be planning to meet the love of your life during a summer vacation. With this scenario, you can understand why you need a completely different wardrobe than in the first scenario.

So as you are developing yours style, you need to think about what you are looking to achieve in your life, and then find a way to incorporate fashion into it as well. This will affect the clothing that you are going to wear, as well as the accessories that you may choose to complete your look.

Become Fashion Literate

You probably think that you know plenty about fashion, but when you are working on developing your personal fashion style, you need to spend some more time looking at the intricacies of fashion. This needs for you to do a little research.

Take the time to lead and differentiate the different designers that exist, such as being able to tell what separates Armani from DKNY for example. This will require you to look at their clothes on the runway or online to understand the differences. By doing this, you will be able to decipher what elements of design that really get you excited.

In addition to being able to differentiate the designers, you also need some knowledge on the fabrics that are available. By touch, you should be able to tell the difference between cotton and silk for example. Over time, you will also need to be able to differentiate blends which have unique attributes such as being wrinkle free. With this knowledge, you will know which fabrics need to be carefully stored, and those that are best for wearing for specific situations.

If you are small and want to use your clothes to help you appear slightly bigger, then you should opt for fabrics that are shiny, or textures which are stiff in nature. With these on, you can still look flattering, while also appearing to be a little larger than you actually are. On the other hand, you have the more common problem, which is wanted to appear slimmer than you are. Wearing clothes that are matte, or those which resemble jersey will help you to appear much slimmer than you are.

As part of yours style development, it helps if you know which clothes and styles are in season at specific times, as these will affect how you dress from one month to the next. Use trends and this information to help you make informed decisions and get inspiration for design and clothing.

Take it A Day at A Time

When you are developing your style, you may think about making a drastic change, by throwing out all of your old clothes and simply replacing them with a whole bunch of new ones. This is something that you should avoid as the aim is to develop yours style, rather than to shock it.

This means that you should start by adding a few small pieces of clothing and accessories that will help you get an idea of your new style direction. You can also consider making changes to some of the clothes that you already have in your wardrobe. For example, you could add some embellishments to a few pairs of jeans to see what they look like, or add accessories to a dress to test how good your feel.

With these tips, you will look and feel as though you have stepped out of the pages of a fashion magazine, even when you are going around to the shop near your home. Once you have developed your style, you will be better able to get the powerful specific pieces that will define the rest of your wardrobe. The rest of these chapters will help you achieve this.

Chapter 4:
Choosing your Personal Style

You have the foundation to start working on your personal style, and now it is time to take this a notch higher and look at the different fashion styles that exist. What is great about fashion is the fact there are so many different things that you can explore, so you do not have to limit yourself to looking just one way. Here are some of the fashion styles that you can refer to for inspiration.

On Trend

This is for the girl who always wants to look like she is in tune with the latest that is happening with fashion in the world. This type of style calls for you to update your wardrobe every season. To keep this up, you need to constantly listen and read fashion news so that you know what you must have on to look as though you have just stepped out of a high fashion magazine.

Vibrant

All eyes are on you if you go with fashions style that can best be described as vibrant. This is a look that is intense, in both color of clothing and design that has been chosen. Here, you will be wearing numerous colors that are meant to draw attention, and have designs which are often asymmetrical in nature. In fact, when people look at what you have on, they may feel as though there is something about your clothing that has been exaggerated for the overall effect.

Casual

Putting clothes together simply, and making it look easy is anything but easy. It actually requires a considerable amount of thought as each piece should make a statement that brings the whole look together. This is what dressing up casual is all about. For the longest time, when one mentioned casual clothing, what would come to mind is people putting on a pair of blue jeans with a white t-shirt. This is not what casual is all about. It needs some coordination to ensure that the entire look comes together well. Typically, a pair of jeans, a loose top, handbag that matches with the shoes and some accessories is the way to go for the casual look.

Elegant

This is the look that you would use to describe glamour. With this look, you are looking at making the most of fashion so that you finish off with a refined outfit that everyone wants to emulate. When someone sees you looking elegant, they will understand that a considerable amount of thought has gone into your look, from the clothing to the accessories, and even the hair and the make-up. Each piece is a statement piece on its own, and you need to compliment your clothing with excellent jewelry. This is a great way to look professional as well as sexy. With elegant clothing, you will be sending a clear message about what you stand for.

Sexy

This is one of the most challenging dressing styles to get right, because there are so many ways that it can go horribly wrong. What you need to aim for is a look that brings out your best in your clothing,flattering your body shape and also bringing out your very best assets. Normally, the parts of the body where one shows skin to be sexy include around the breasts, the legs and the stomach. For a sexy style, you can choose to wear short skirts or dresses which cover and follow every curve on your body. Normally, you will have high heels on your feet as these will elongate your les. For a daring look, you can try out something that is low cut to amplify your breasts.

Exotic

You do not need to remain within the confines of your culture when you are looking at putting together an outfit. For your personal style, you can draw inspiration from a range of other cultures. Perhaps you want to go with the bold colors and sparkly elements that you will find within Asian inspired clothing, or the bright prints that you would get from African inspired clothing. Either way, if you are going for an exotic look, you are looking at doing something with yours style that other people around you have not mastered yet. This is what you should do if you want to have pieces that are quite eye catching, and which will ensure that you are never missed when amongst a crowd.

Girly

There are girls who love to wear pink, look soft and feminine at all times and this is the look that you can achieve if you go for the girly edge as part of your style. Typically, you will find that there are clothes which are made with plenty of ruffles and lace, as well as elements that are quite girly including hearts and flowers. Most of the clothing that is girly uses colors that are best described as soft, such as pastel colors, and of course, various shades of light pink as well as white. This look is whimsical and romantic, and can add an element of youth to any woman's personal style.

Preppy

If you are living in a town that is surrounded by college students, you may find yourself wanting to look more like them and getting wardrobe inspiration in this way. That is what looking preppy is all about. This is the sort of look where you will put on dark tights underneath a short skirt, and have a sweater on top with white sleeves poking out of the bottom. It is meant to look comfortable and cute. To finish off the look, you may even decide to wear some clear glasses, and to have your hair in a messy bun. The aim of this look is to make the most of numerous pieces, as well as to look practical.

Artsy

This is a style that is completely off trend and individual. A person that is artsy may find they are most comfortable in clothes like cutoff jeans and cotton shirts. To bring the look together, one may accessorize with hats, bags, jackets or even suspenders. As an individual style, it differs from one person to the next, though when you look at it, you will easily be able to identify the style for what it is and what it represents.

Boho Chic

There are numerous actresses and other famous people who love this way of dressing. Boho chic style draws its inspiration from the seventies, where loose clothing in amazing shapes was the talk of the town. Today, it embodies clothing that has interesting patterns on it, as well as a range of textures. It is best suited for those who want to be identified as hippies or even gypsies due to the elements that are needed to put an outfit together. There are designs such as the fabulous tie dye design, as well as things like fringes which only add to the total appeal of an outfit.

Cow Girl

Immediately you think about this style, there are some items that will spring into your mind. At the peak would be some blue jeans that are boot cut, together with some excellent boots to match. At the top, a nice shirt with a beautiful color, well-fitting on the body, and a pretty hat for a cowgirl. This is the type of style that you would be bringing forward if you choose to dress in this way. It is a classic look that always looks great, and can easily be accessorized with a host of belts, necklaces and bags. It appears to be easy to wear and will make your efforts at style appear to be simple and smooth.

Punk

For distinct style that will ensure you get noticed in a crowd, you should try out punk fashion. This style will let everyone know that you are in the building, as it has a considerable amount of attitude associated with it. There are certain fabrics that you will find in this style more than in a host of other styles. These include a range of plaid designs, which are normally in dark colors. In addition, you will also find that there is quite a bit of leather, as well as chains and spikes. This is a style that is best suited for anyone who wants to make a bold statement and be truly unforgettable.

Gothic

This look is a little different from the punk looking, though they are often mistaken for being similar. This is because they are both looks that make a bold statement, and this statement veers towards a dark look. For the most part, gothic clothing is black in color, and this includes the hair and accessories that are worn as well. This clothes for the most part are tight, and also worn in layers with a large amount of accessorized. When you see someone dressed in this style, you may believe that there is something mysterious and fascinating about them and want to know them a little more.

Professional

There is a distinct look that a professional woman should don, and that is embodied by different pieces which are classic and timeless in their design. This look will call for a range of suits within your wardrobe, which should help you look great. With this look, you will be easily respected. Your wardrobe will include a range of blazers, panty hose and pencil skirts to ensure that you can keep it up.

Sporty

This is the girl who will step out in yoga pants, a sweatshirt and a pair of sneakers. The look communicates that the wearer is ready for action, whether this be hitting the gym or going for a run. It is not in any way fashionable and does not have the same flash or talk ability of some of the other styles, though it is a comfortable style that will easily stand the test of time.

There are so many different styles that you can find, and knowing how they are distinct from each other will help you choose the one that best suits you.

Chapter 5:
Work with Accessories

The easiest way to elevate any outfit is to accessorize, though it is important that you know how to accessorize. Fashion accessories include handbags, hats, shoes, belts, jewelry, socks and ornaments to wear in your hair. The guidelines that you consider when picking accessories are similar to those of choosing your basic outfit. You should understand how accessories help to define your personal style and make you look chic. This is what your accessories are communicating: -

- **Glamour** – Rings with large stones, huge sunglasses, chandelier earrings and six-inch heels communicate that your personal style is glamorous.

- **Casual** – Bright colored layered bracelets, handbags with long straps and gladiator sandals are great for casual wear.

- **Classics** – An expensive silk scarf, simple black pumps, and pearl stud earrings are classic items that have stood the test of time for expressing chic taste and style.

- **Playful** – Cross body hobo bags, thin belts, chunky jewelry and flat shoes express a playful nature.

- **Work** – When at the office, you can wear a classic watch, kitten heels, and simple necklace. These items are not distracting, and people will pay more attention to what you doing than what you are wearing.

- **Unique** – There are accessories that simply make you stand out from the crowd. These could include studded leather boots or a tight choker. If you want to define yourself as chic, then these types of accessories will give you a more urban look.

With accessories, it is possible to accentuate your very best features, while minimizing those that you do not like, or which do not flatter your body in any way. In addition, they have the ability to revitalize any outfit, even one that has been in your wardrobe for several seasons. It is accessories that will cement your chic look and finish off your outfit.

Here are some essential tips to help you work with accessories:

Dressing Up Prints

Outfits that contain prints are strong in the statement that you express, and you would be making a mistake if you wore bright and bold accessories with them. There are so many different prints that you can find. Some of the most famous and iconic are pinstripes, or polka dots. There are other types of prints including animal prints, floral prints, geometric shape prints and ethnic prints. There are prints which appear to be delicate and with intricate detail, while others are very bold and seem to make an unforgettable statement.

When your outfit is powerful and expressive in the print, it is better to go for simple accessories. The reason being if you wear anything complex, you lessen the chic factor of your outfit. Simple accessories such as a plain gold bracelet, or a bag that is one color, are ideal for a pattered outfit. These can often be of any width or length, just as long as they do not seem to be overpowering your outfit,

On the other hand, you may have a print that is very delicate in its nature. For these, it is better to wear accessories that are minimalist in nature so as not to overpower the core outfit that is already there. Thin chains and charm bracelets can really lock in the style that you need with these types of prints.

If you have on a geometric or animal print, you can choose to wear accessories that pick up on the colors in your print, which will help to emphasize it more.

Selecting a Bag

There are numerous types of bags, and the variations may be in the materials that they are made with, the size of the bag, the way that it is worn and so on. The size of your bag, as well as its shape, are what you will consider when choosing an accessory. You also need to consider your body shape, as tall women are better suited to smaller bags like clutches and shorter women look good with handbags that have short straps and are medium sizes. If you are curvy, then a handbag that is boxed shape will help to balance your curves rather than to over-accentuate them.

Bags are also made from a range of materials, and most of them are seasonal. This means that it is better and more economical to consider what is in the market, and then choose a bag based on this. Most people will have a black leather bag due to its versatility and ability to clean with ease.

You may also find that you can get a bag that is made of cloth for more casual looks, and this can easily be slung over your shoulder. There are also bags that resemble baskets which you can wear when you are going for some shopping, or those which are bedazzled with jewels which are ideal for an elegant night out.

When looking at bags, it is good to have some staples, and some quirky choices. Wearing a bag allows you to take on some risk with your outfits, without worrying that you may take your look to far and then ruin an entire outfit.

Brighten Up Dark Colors

To create an outfit that makes a statement, you should choose accessories that brighten up dark colors. For example, consider you have a plain black pair of trousers, matched with a black shirt as your base outfit. To accessorize, you could choose to wear a bright mint green tote bag, a gold and enamel bracelet and some mint green and black high heeled shoes. The green accessories match with the black dress and are simple and stylish. The enamel bracelet has a little gold, which is known to make any outfit look chic. What could have been a dull outfit that communicated nothing is transformed into art with bright accessories.

In addition, you should avoid wearing a range of dark colors together. Think about how strange and dark it would look for you to wear some black trousers and a navy jacket. If you have a dark color, you can wear it in different shades so that you get the best possible look from it.

When you use accessories properly, you will find that one base layer of clothing can create lots of different looks. This is a smart way to extend your wardrobe and make fashion easier to understand, while also helping you to save money.

Accessory Don'ts!

One thing that you should note is that you do not wear too many accessories at one time. You need a statement piece, and perhaps one to two more accessories. To look chic, you must remember that less is, in fact, more. Therefore, do not attempt to dress up an outfit with jewelry, a scarf, sunglasses, a hat and more without considering the time of day and where you may be going with that outfit. Doing this will completely overshadow your outfit as the accessories may end up competing for attention, which will make you appear unpolished.

Also, avoid trying to match every element of your outfit. Consider that you are wearing a black dress with red flowers. You do not need to wear red earrings, red shoes and carry a red bag. To be chic, you should change it up and try color blocking instead. Color blocking occurs when you have a range of accessories that have bold and different colors and add an interesting touch to plain outfits.

If you are confused about what colors match well, you can refer to the famous color wheel. This wheel features primary and secondary colors. When two colors are next to each other, they will make a god match as they often differ in their level of lightness. In addition, colors that are opposite each other make a bold statement as well as a sharp contrast, and look great together.

As you try and decide how to accessorize, remember that you do not need to limit yourself to the accessories that have been mentioned so far. Go outside the box and choose other items that add chic to your outfit. A small umbrella may be the perfect accessory for your trench coat and trouser outfit, especially in wet weather. When you are going out in the evening, you may opt for a chic fur coat or feather boa. It is essential that you remain open minded to the different items available, as this will help you better express your own individual chic.

Chapter 6:
Finding the Right Shoes

Sometimes, the only article of clothing that you need to really define your style is an amazing pair of shoes. There are numerous types and styles that are available, but when it comes to style, there are those that you must have as the base in your wardrobe so that you are ready to face any occasion. Here are some pieces that you should stock up on,

Black Pumps

These are shoes that can wear many hats from being practical and going with almost any clothing, to also being very sexy and feminine. They are timeless in their design, often featuring a high heel, with the front of the shoe tapering off into a triangle at the toe. It is possible to wear these shoes on a daily basis as they will always add an element of sophistication to any outfit. Almost all fashion designers have their own take of these shoes.

Nude Pumps

Like the black pump, you also need to have a pair of nude pumps in your wardrobe, especially if you are looking to ensure that you have some dressy shoes for when you are at work. These are excellent shoes for any woman who is not very tall, as when you wear them, the effect is elongating your legs and making you appear as though you have much more height than usual. They are classic in their nature, and are also highly versatile. The color of these shoes is neutral, which makes it possible to wear them with almost any clothing.

High Heeled Sandals

When you want to look elegant, and are looking for the perfect styled shoes to match with any clothing, whether trousers or a dress, then you should slip on a pair of high heeled sandals. These types of shoes look relatively formal, and are ideal for wearing to events that take place in the evenings. You need to ensure that you have well pedicured feet and polished toes in order to really pull of his look.

Espadrilles

There are few shoes that will remind you of summer clothing and style as much as a pair of espadrilles. These shoes are typically high heels, though different as they are in wedge form. The heel is then covered with rope and the top may have straps of be closed in the front. This means that you can achieve both an open and a closed tow look with these shoes on. They are easy to wear and walk around in as they require less balance than a high heel. If you want to create a look that is fun, and still retains a certain amount of elegance within it, then this is the perfect shoe for you to go for.

Oxfords

Most women will have a wide range of high heeled shoes in their wardrobes, though it may not be practical to always keep these shoes on. For this reason, you need to have a sensible pair of flat shoes for other occasions. Flat shoes do not have to be boring or mono-toned. For a sense of style, you should include a pair of Oxfords in your wardrobe, or some comfortable loafers. These will make you look great, while also ensuring that you retain sophistication with any outfit that you are wearing. These types of flat shoes are known as menswear-inspired, and can be worn for the entire day without any issue.

Doll Shoes

These are flat beautiful shoes that are designed to follow the shape of your toes and simply to slip them on. They are highly versatile and so comfortable, that you may not even feel as though you have some shoes on your feet. You can easily match them with a range of outfits, including dresses, skirts and trousers. They are available with a wide range of embellishments, so you can find some that have cute chic bows, or others that feature buckles and other similar elements.

D'orsay Flats

These are flats with a difference, and will clearly ensure that you are able to stand out when you are in any crowd. They are great if you need to do a considerable amount of walking, as they really allow your foot to breath. By design, these shoes will have a front section, as well as a section to keep your heel in place. In between, the shoe is open, giving the idea that you have somehow managed to put two shoes together. They are an excellent choice for office wear as they will help you to look quite polished and professional when you have them on.

Flat Boots

Style also needs to go with the seasons, especially when you are looking at getting yourself some shoes. During the seasons where there is a large amount of rain, it is typical for shoes to become flatter and closer to the ground so as to minimize the risk of falling and injury. This is when you need yourself a stunning pair of flat boots. A classic black or brown would be a great addition to your wardrobe due to the versatility of wearing these colors, though you could opt for any color that you have clothes to match with.

Simple Sneakers

The average wardrobe should include shoes that can be worn when a person needs to step out and get some exercise. These need to be practical, and can also be a reflection of your own style. Rather than opting for the run off the mill sneakers, which will typically have laces and a sporty sole, one can get themselves a simple pair of slip on sneakers, which also make an excellent fashion statement. These are the shoes that you should consider wearing when you need to give your feet some relief from always being in high shoes. They are practical, and look great.

Chapter 7:
Wardrobe Essentials

When it comes to fashion and building up your wardrobe, there are items that are fads, meaning that they come and go with the changing times. However, there are also some wardrobe items which are essential, as they have been able to stand the test of time for decades. These main pieces of clothing are the focus in this section, as you will often use them as the foundation to create your perfect outfit. You probably already have some of these items, but if you do not, now is the time to go out and get them. They include the following: -

The Little Black Dress

This is a wardrobe staple that was made famous by the chic, and stylish Audrey Hepburn is the Little Black Dress. What is brilliant about this wardrobe staple is that you can choose a shape and design that is suited to your body. This type of dress has minimal to no embellishments, and should be of medium length.

This is an essential item because it can be dressed up or down depending on the occasion. For a night out, you can wear some glittering accessories, a pair of stockings and high heeled shoes to match the dress. For a day at the office, you can layer this dress with a smart, tailored blazer, and some comfortable kitten heels. It is a versatile item that will stand the test of time.

The White T-Shirt

A plain white t-shirt is a must have in your wardrobe as it can form the base for all manner of outfits. Many people believe that a t-shirt does not express any chic, but this is not the case. Consider dressing up a plain white t-shirt with a monochrome ruffle skirt. If you tuck the t-shirt in, and wear some expressive accessories, this t-shirt will appear to be the canvas that enables you to express yourself freely. A white t-shirt is excellent casual chic wear.

Blue Skinny Jeans

Jeans have come a long way since they were first invented for miners by Levi Strauss. Today, they are fashionable items that are so versatile they can be worn for all occasions. Every wardrobe needs a pair of well fitting, dark blue skinny jeans. This is one type of denim trouser that is able to flatter anyone, no matter what their body shape may be. For the best effect, you should have a little bit of stretch in your jeans, so that it sits better on your body.

You can go casual with skinny jeans by wearing a loose bohemian top and rope wedges as accessories, or you can smarten them up with a crisp colored blazer, a beaded necklace and a pair of high-heeled boots. If possible, you should have another two or three pairs of colored jeans as staples in your wardrobe.

Fitting Black Trousers

Every wardrobe needs a pair of well-fitting black trousers, preferably those that stop at your ankles. The fabric that these are made from is important, as they should be soft and comfortable, able to be worn in any weather. Preferably, they should be made from some type of wool that is able to sit on the body well.

The Pencil Skirt

So far, you know that you need some classic black, white and blue items in your wardrobe to help create winning looks. The pencil skirt is another item that you cannot afford to do without. An excellent color for a pencil skirt is grey, as this can easily match with an array of multi-colored items. It is an expression of chic, and a classic that always makes a show stopping statement.

The Wrap Dress

It was over forty years ago that the legendary creative fashion designer Diane von Furstenberg designed the iconic wrap dress. It remains a stable item in almost all wardrobes to this day. This is a highly versatile essential item, which can easily be dressed up or down. It is also able to flatter almost any figure, and is instantly recognizable. For simple fashion that works every time you wear it, you need to ensure that you have one of these in your wardrobe.

The Neutral Trench Coat

This is a wardrobe essential that can easily be placed over any type of outfit to complete a look. Trench coats are often waterproof meaning that you can wear them in any weather. In addition, they are well structure so that they bring out your best features. A neutral color is able to match with virtually anything you put on, whether it is plain or has a print.

A Tailored Blazer

Wearing a blazer is an excellent way to flatter your silhouette, but that is only if it is fitting you well. When a blazer is ill fitting, it makes your entire outfit appear dowdy and careless. The parts that need to fit like a glove are the shoulders as well as the sleeves. To achieve this perfect fit, it is better to have a blazer that has been tailored to fit your body to perfection, rather than to compromise and purchase a blazer that does not deliver everything that you need. Blazers are excellent for wearing to the office or meetings, and also for dressing up an outfit when going out in the evening.

Black Pumps

Wardrobe essentials extend beyond clothes and also include accessories. Black pumps should be a stable in every wardrobe as they can be worn at any time of day or night. They can complete an outfit for the work place, as well as add a classic finish to an evening dress. These are an excellent fashion stable if you want to be identified with chic taste and style.

Diamond or Pearl Studs

Nothing says chic and put together like a beautiful pair of diamond and pearl studs. This is one tiny accessory that has the power to speak volumes when included in an outfit. You do not need to find real diamonds, in case you immediately started to worry about your budget. Wear a pair of faux diamonds or pearls instead, and you will look chic and classy wherever you are.

Bright, Red Lipstick

Anyone looking to express themselves as having chic taste, will polish off their overall look with a powerful and expressive red lipstick. You do not need to go for the brightest shade of red that you can find so that you are seen from afar. Instead, you need to understand your own skin tone, so that you can find a shade of red that matches perfectly. To express chic, you should purchase a matte lipstick rather than a glossy one.

Cool Sunglasses

A pair of fantastic sunglasses is the icing on the cake, or the last element that can bring your entire outfit together. Before you purchase any sunglasses, you need to understand the shape of your face so that you can pick a pair that is flattering. Rather than opting for sunglasses that are on trend, you should seek some favorites that have stood the test of time. An excellent option that seems to suit almost everyone are a pair of aviators, the signature sunglasses from maker, Ray Ban.

Black Iconic Handbag

Every woman needs to have an iconic handbag that will stand the test of time, and be ideal for wearing at any time with almost any outfit. This will typically mean that you need to invest in a handbag, as getting that iconic look is best achieved with a designer piece.

There are bags like the 2.55 from Chanel, or the Hermes Birkin Bag that is made by hand and with a considerable amount of care. In addition to being instantly recognizable as a style element, these are bags that will last you for years, and which will never go out of style. That is what having something chic in your wardrobe is all about.

Overall, you can get away with an excellent wardrobe if you remember that you need some variety, and control over the number of pieces that you own. Ensure that you have all the essentials to begin with, as this will enable you to wear a range of outfits. Then, you need a few patterned items. For a chic look, the best pattern that you can have in your wardrobe is leopard print. Finally, you need to purchase at least two outfits that are total showstoppers. These are what you will turn to when you have to dress up for a special occasion.

Chapter 8:
Dress for your Shape

The beauty of the world and the people in it is their unique and distinct differences. As you select the items that you want to wear to express yourself, you will realize that you must consider the shape of your body. Clothes are made to fit within certain body shapes, so once you understand what your shape is, you will be able to pick out the most flattering clothing. Use your clothing to accentuate the parts of your body that you like the most.

Begin by determining your actual size using three main choices which are small, medium and large. The scientific way of establishing which size you are would involve an evaluation of both your height and your weight. A shortcut requires you to measure using your hand and your wrist.

To confirm your size, hold the arm which you use to write out. Using your other hand, wrap your thumb and index finger around the wrist, being careful to position your fingers just below the wrist bone. If the fingers are able to touch easily, or if they have an overlap, then it means you are small. If they are barely touching, then you are medium. If they are not touching at all, and have a distance of one centimeter or more between them, it is an indication that you are large.

Understanding the size of your body is important when you need to choose accessories to match with your outfits. If you are small, then the accessories that you choose should be small to medium. If you are medium, the same applies, especially if you are also short. If you are large, then you need medium to large accessories, although if you happen to be short as well, then you should use accessories that are small to medium.

The most flattering shape that a woman could have is the hourglass figure, where the body goes in at the waist and the bust and hips flare out attractively. If you do not have this figure, it is highly likely that the close you choose to wear will be helping you create an illusion of an hourglass figure. Consider the following shapes.

Triangle or Inverted Triangle

If your body shape is like a triangle, it means that you have wide hips and an inverted triangle means your upper body and bust are wide. With the triangle shape, your waist will be defined, and you likely have a rounded bottom and flat stomach. The best way to dress this type of shape is to use layering. For a triangle shape, your layers will be focused on the top half of your body as you work towards increasing the overall width of your shoulders so that you look balanced. This can be done by choosing clothes which have sleeves or wearing colors that are brighter on the top than on the bottom. On the bottom half of your body, you can draw attention away from your wider hips by ensuring that items have wide hems and are dark in color.

With an inverted triangle shape, your focus will be on increasing the width of your hips which you can accomplish by wearing bright colored bottoms, like an A-line skirt. People who have this body shape usually have beautiful legs as well, so it would be worth showing them off by wearing items that are a little short. To help create some balance, you can dress this shape in wide leg pants or styles which have high waists. This will help with creating the illusion of an existing waist.

Rectangle Shape

If you have a rectangle shape, then it means that your body does not go in at the waist, rather, it appears to be completely straight from your bust down to your hips. People with this type of figure tend to appear as more athletic in nature. The clothes that you choose should work towards giving your waist some definition. Rather than wearing tight and fitting clothes, and creating a waist by using belts for example, it is better to wear something that flows and skims over the entire body. This is ideal for a dress. If you are wearing separates, it is better to have tops that stop just below the waist, as this gives some more definition.

You can also choose tops that have sweetheart necklines or scoop necks as these help to create the illusion of curves. Ruching can also ensure great results, as are clothes which have ruffles or extra details at the top and bottom.

Apple Shape

Your shape may be round all over, meaning that you do not have a defined waist as most of your weight is carried around your mid-section. This also means that quite often, your hips are narrow and you have nice, well defined legs. In that case, to flatter your shape you need to avoid clothes which attract attention to your waist. Empire waistlines that stop just below the bust line are very flattering, as are longer tops that are loose at the top, and come together above the knees.

This kind of shape also does well with looks with are monochromatic. To make the torso look longer and this create a waist, V-neck tops are an excellent choice. To make the most of your legs, you can dress in a skirt as this will take away attention from your mid-section, which many people with this shape do not find flattering.

Hourglass Shape

This is the body shape that almost everyone is working to attain, though you must be careful how you dress this shape up so that you remain looking chic rather than trashy. What you want to do is accentuate your whole body, as you have the right shape from head to toe. Your shoulders and hips are quite close in size, and then you have a tiny waist to boot.

With this figure, you would look great in a pair of skinny jeans with a fitted white button down shirt, or in the iconic wrap dress. You can also afford to show off your hips in clothes which have high waists, and are made from an array of light fabrics.

If you are tall, and have legs that go on for days, you can accentuate them by wearing short skirts or daisy duke shorts. This will make them look longer, and show them off beautifully.

Finishing Off the Face

An important part of getting dressed up for your shape is also ensuring that you dress your face up as well. So far, the essential make-up item that has been mentioned to help achieve a flawless chic look is a brilliant red lipstick. There is so much more that you can do though.

Your regime should begin by creating an ideal foundation. To do this, you need to start by using a satin finish foundation to even out your skin tone, and follow this with a concealer.

Then, pat your face down with a loose powder and finish off your cheekbones with a bronzer.

Next, you should move on to your eyes. Chic makeup will have you appear to have wide and attractive doe eyes. This helps you look approachable and confident. You will begin with an eyeshadow that is lighter than your skin tone, and cover your eyelid with this. Then add a shade that is slightly darker to the crease, and use a dark liquid liner to line the eyes. Try and avoid a black eye liner as this tends to look harsh. It would be better to use an eyeliner that is dark brown in color. At the inner rim of your eye, use some white eyeliner and they will instantly open out. Add two layers of quality mascara and finish off by shaping your eyebrows. Chic makeup rarely uses bold and loud colors. It is more about accentuating the eyes using subtlety.

If you want to go beyond the red lipstick and experiment, you should do so with dark shades of lipstick. These give an appearance of chic much more effectively that bright shades.

Chapter 9:
Remember Your Face

In the last section, a quick fix for finishing off your face with an outfit was described. This will give you the basic chic look. This section looks at this more deeply, starting off with what you will do to your hair, and then moving this on to include your face. As you take the time to watch what is happening in the world of fashion, especially when it comes to watching runway shows, you will find that as much attention is paid to the hair and makeup as is given to the clothing that the models are wearing. This is because your face is the polish of your entire outfit, and you need to pay as much attention to detail as you can when you are looking to achieve a stunning overall look. Here are a few chic things that you can do with your hair.

The Fishtail Braid

There is the traditional braid which is what your parents possibly did to your hair when you were a little girl, then you have the more sophisticated fishtail braid which is the epitome of looking and being chic.

The fishtail braid can be left down for a simple boho-chic look, or you could make it more elegant by having it as part of a glamourous up do. It can be worn both day and night with ease.

You can also use this style to create a number of braids around your head, which you can then style in various ways to give yourself a look that will help you resemble a Grecian goddess.

The Faux Bob

If you have long locks and are looking to achieve a chic bob for a dinner event, there is no need for you to get some scissors out and chop off all your hair. Instead, you could opt to put up a faux bob. Typically, you will start out by having all of your hair curled and then you can simply run through it with your fingers. Then, you hold your hair in a low pony tail below the nape of your neck. Gently bend in the ponytail and tuck it underneath the nape of your neck, pinning it into place.

The Traditional Bun

Most people know how to turn their hair around into a traditional bun. However, there is so much more that you can do to a bun when you want to appear more chic. You could first braid your hair and then put it into a burn, or hold it into a ponytail, curl it all up, and then put it into a bun.

Once you have managed to do something with your hair, you can begin to do something with your face to achieve a chic look. Chic making and style is minimalist, which means that it is barely there, but enough to make you look different. You need to go through various stages to get the look right. Here is how you can begin.

The Base

The first thing that you will need to do is even out your entire skin tone. This requires you to start with some foundation, working from the middle of your face and then moving out towards the rest of your face. There are areas on your face which will be uneven, where you can use some cream concealer. This is often around the eyes and will ensure that if you have dark under eyes, you can maintain the same color on the rest of your face. Set your entire face with some loose powder that is translucent. For the final part of the base, use some bronzer on your cheeks. This will help make your face look much slimmer than normal.

When you have this base, it will be much easier to build on to it. If you want to appear more rosy in the cheeks due to having pale skin, then you can substitute the bronzer with blusher for a stunning result.

The Eyes

The next part of your face that you will need to work on is your eyes. What you want is to open up the eyes as much as possible, without doing anything too extreme with your eye make-up. To do this, you should begin by making use of an eye shadow that is a little lighter than your actual skin and spreading this all across your eyelid. You can then apply a shade that is a little darker on your crease, as this will help your eyes to look bigger than they are.

If you are looking at working with some other shades of eyeshadow, you need to go with some pastel colors, and then ensure that they are as matte as possible. Having a matte look ties in better to being chic than having a look that is glittery or shiny.

The next thing that you need to use is a black eye liner, which you need to help define your lash line. This line should be thin and as close to the lash line as possible, though it can thicken a little bit as you move closer to the outer edge of your eye. If you find that the black eyeliner is too harsh and dark for your skin tone, you may choose instead to make use of a brown eyeliner which can give you a much gentler look.

On your eyelashes, you should apply some mascara, with the best black thickening mascara being an excellent option. A maximum of two coats should be used on the upper lashes, and you can use on coat on the lower lashes. If you are blessed with thick eyelashes, you may choose to use some clear mascara instead. This is because the heavy lashes may make your eyes appear much heavier and darker than they really are, which could possibly close your eyes rather than have them appear as open as you would like.

To finish off your eyes, you need to work on your eyebrows. This requires you to shape them with an eyebrow powder which should be as close in color to your hair as is possible. If you are not sure about how you can shape your eyebrows for the best result, you could make use of an eyebrow stencil shaper which will help you achieve the shape that you need without worry that one brow will look different from the other.

The Lips

Now, you can work on the next defining feature on your face which is the lips. You need to begin by choosing a neutral shade, or if you want to go a little bolder, a color that appears to be more like a stain than a bold color. To start you will trace out your lip using a lip color that is the same shade. Once your lip has been fully lined, you should fill it in with your lip color., This will help your color to stay on for longer and prevent bleeding which can make you look messy and take away from your sophisticated look overall.

There are different types of lipsticks that are available, including both glossy and matte looks. Both of these can fit into being chic, depending on when and how they are worn. If you have a glossy lipstick, it would be better suited to being worn in the morning or in the evening for a formal look. In the middle of the day if attending a casual event, then the matte look would work much better and should be worn instead.

Your Nails

Finally, the last part of your look, although it is not part of your face, is your nails. These will make a massive impact on what you look like at the end. You need to have a professional manicure and pedicure done so that you can look your best. Choose a color that can easily match up with most of your clothing, and keep it on for around a week to avoid the chips that can look quite unsightly as a part of your look.

In addition, be mindful of the length of your nails when you want to wear. The chic look does not have long nails that resemble talons. When you want to look like you have style and are chic, then you can have length that are slightly long, and oval or square in their shape. A classic way to ensure that you are able to maintain that chic look is by getting yourself a French manicure. This is what will help you look amazing.

Part of bringing together your style, is ensuring that you are able to take care of your total look, from head to toe. Looking chic and expressing your style requires all the possible input that you can use.

Chapter 10:
Do Not Cramp Your Style

As you continue on this journey of style, you may find that you get inspiration to try all sorts of looks from the red carpet or even from magazines. Although these are the go to sources to get a great look, you also need to ensure that you do not just settle for the first look that you come across. The people who come up with these looks are typically human and may also come up with looks that are far from practical, and which will not help you elevate your own personal style. In the spirit of making sure that you look your very best at all times, here are some things that you should avoid so as not to cramp your style.

Reading Glasses

Glasses are an excellent accessory, if worn right. There are certain looks that are effortlessly on trend, such as sunglasses in various shapes and designs. One of the looks that should be avoided if you want to maintain any sense of style if wearing reading glasses when you are walking around. In addition, you need to avoid having your reading glasses hanging off a chain around your neck. Use them for their primary purpose. If you do need glasses to see, that is different, as you can always get a pair with a frame that is suited to your face.

Tweed Suits

These were once made famous by designer Coco Chanel, but that was a long time ago. Now, if you wear these suits and the cut is not right, you run the risk of looking much older than you really are. This is a sure fire way to cramp your personal style. If you do want to wear a pattern that resembles tweed, you can go for something that is equally iconic, such a hound's tooth.

Mom Jeans

When you are looking for clothing that puts comfort first, above all style, then you are likely going to slip into a pair of mom jeans. Please, do not do this. Mom Jeans can also be described as jeans that have an incredibly high waist, and at the bottom take on a peg leg shape. They typically do not flatter any body type, and will hang loosely where they are supposed to hold on to the body. With so many different designs for jeans being available, these need to be avoided as much as possible.

Socks

They are meant to keep your feet warm, or to protect them when you are doing sport. That is the role of socks. If you want to avoid cramping your style, avoid putting on socks when you are wearing high heels, or if you are wearing anything on your feet other than sneakers. This will take away from a carefully thought out look, and make you appear quite immature.

Old Items

There is a world of different between old clothes and vintage clothes. Old clothes are simply those that have been in your wardrobe for a long time, and that you have not been able to wear. This means that they are likely to have become worn with time, and may have even lost their richness in color. However, it is possible to get some vintage items which you can wear. These are clothes which were made long time ago, though they had such excellent quality and care, that they have stood the test of time. These clothes are what will help you bring out your personal style, much more than the clothes that you have simply kept for a long time. If you are purchasing vintage clothing because that is the style that you want to emulate, look for classics like Chanel suits, or some Valentino dresses.

When it comes to style, there is quite a bit that you can do, and things that you can get away with which do not interfere with your look. There are also some things that you need to avoid, and these are at the top of the list. With all the hard work that you are doing to develop your style, you should make sure that you do not do something small that will have a negative impact on all of your hard work so far.

Chapter 11:
Dressing for Your Day

This section shall take you through an entire day, giving you guidance on how you can achieve three main looks, from the morning look, afternoon look and evening look. This way, you can confidently choose a look that will flatter you for the entire day.

The Morning Look

The most challenging part of putting together an outfit in the morning is figuring out what you should wear for the day. This can be a frustrating process that has you throw on whatever you can find in frustration. Here are the steps that you can follow to make the process much more bearable.

1. **Make a decision early**

   If it takes you ages to decide what you are going to where, start thinking about it from the moment that you get out of bed. This means that while you are in the shower, have a checklist in your mind of the outfit you want to put together. Think about what you need to accomplish by the end of the day, and start narrowing your decisions from this perspective.

2. **Think about the weather**

   Consider what is happening with the weather, so that you know what is appropriate for the entire day. If it is a cold day, you may want to layer on some of your clothing so that you keep warm during the day, and can easily get lighter when the weather warms up. For a hot day, you may choose a fabric that is light and airy.

3. Have some extra time

When you are going to watch a football match, you are often prepared for the game to go into extra time if there is no clear winner by the end. You need to consider having some extra time in the morning, just in case it takes you sometime to get ready. When you run short of time, you tend to rush and make decisions that are not rational. Ensure you have about fifteen additional minutes to help you deal with any indecisiveness.

4. Consider Options

Try not to put all your eggs in one basket, by thinking about trying on only one outfit. Have at least two to three outfits in mind so that you do not have to rummage through your wardrobe if your primary option does not work out.

5. Try Something On

You will only know whether you want to wear something after you have tried it on and assessed the outfit. Make sure that you have plenty of time to evaluate your options, and have fully accessorized your clothing so that you have something on that you are proud of.

6. Pick your Outfit the Night Before

If you really want to avoid the drama that goes into picking an outfit on a daily basis, then you need to ensure that you have selected the outfit the night before. This way, you can confidently wake up in the morning sure that you will look great for the day. What's even better is that you can try all your options on in no rush the night before, helping you make a simple dressing decision.

The Afternoon Get Together

Normally in the afternoon, you may need to change your outfits for a casual get together with friends. This is perhaps the easiest time of day to dress for as you do not need to be too formal, neither do you need to ensure that you do not have a hair out of place. You can be much freer with your look at this time. Here are the rules to follow: -

1. The Type of Dress

Dresses that are worn in the middle of the day are much less fussy and complex than dresses worn at other times of the day. At this time of day, you can wear dresses that stop above the knee, or those which are much shorter depending on the occasion. You need to keep your dress as simple as possible, and also ensure that you look like a lady. This is when you can look to wear prints that are very bold, or those which have lady like elements including flowers and other designs.

2. The Color of Your Dress

Since you are meant to look light and airy, then the color of your dress is equally versatile. Ideally, if you will be wearing a print, you should ensure that the base color on that print is white, or that you can easily match your outfit up with something white.

The best shades to go for if you want full color are those which are light and airy. These tend to be more fun, and more free for one to wear. As long as you are able to simplify any design that seems to be too bold, you will find that you can wear any design that you like.

3. Manage your Accessories

You should avoid falling into the trap of putting on too many accessories. This is when you need to have statement pieces more than anything else. This means that if you are wearing a necklace, you can make sure that it is a big one with lots of character. This also goes for bracelets, earrings and the like. You can also wear a pair of matching handbags and shoes. Since you are dressing for day time, try and avoid wearing items that are too sparkly and shiny as these are better suited for wearing during the night time.

4. Hats and Things

There are few occasions where a hat is as appropriate as during the afternoon, so this is when you should experience this fashion accessory. You can try out different styles and colors of hats as they can completely transform an outfit and help you look spectacular.

The Evening Look

Normally in the evenings, you may need to get dressed to attend an event or something that is far more dressy and formal than the typical day at work. For this reason, you also need some smarts when it comes to choosing that perfect evening outfit. Mostly, one would select a dress to wear on special occasions, though it is also possible to find some smart trouser suits. Make your decision considering the following: -

1. Style

You will find numerous styles available for an evening gown and it is up to you to choose a style that will really stand the test of time. This means that you should have some evening looks in your wardrobe that are best described as classics. They should have enough elegance to ensure that you stand out, yet be discreet enough in their design to be worn more than once with different accessories.

2. Your Body Shape

Where possible, you should get an evening dress that will be tailored to fit your body. This is because everyone has a different body shape and for you to look spectacular, you need the dress to choose you perfectly.

Your body shape will also have an impact on the length of the dress. Ideally, you should choose a gown which is a dress that will go all the way down to your ankles. Alternatively, you may choose a shorter option which stops above the knee. For both options, a pair of high heels will really help to bring forth your best features. As a rule of thumb, the more formal the event, the longer the dress you need to wear. Also, make sure that you are not showing off your underwear at any time. If you are a little larger, you may have to be careful about the underwear that you wear beneath the dress so that you do not have any tell tall lines showing up.

3. The Function You Are Attending

Once you have considered your body shape, then you need think about the function you are attending. This will determine who risqué your outfit is going to be, and the types of accessories that you will wear. Accessories in this case include your hair and makeup, as well as your jewelry and the shoes that you will have on.

Also, consider that in the function you are attending, you do not want to be the person that looks as though they are out of place. You need to ensure that you blend in with other people, and also express that you have some class as well as fashion sense.

4. Picking the Right Color

The most popular colors for evening dresses are black and red, though you do not need to restrict yourself to these two fabulous colors. There is no need for you to look safe every time that you are going out for a formal occasion in the evening. You can choose a dress in a color that suits your complexion. If you have a complexion that is peachy, you can wear a dress with a dark red undertone. If you are wearing a dress that is wine colored, you should have a complexion that is warm in its nature.

5. Comfort

Finally, think about how comfortable that you are going to be. You need to ensure that you are able to walk easily, to sit down and to dance if necessary. This means that you should not wear a dress that is too restrictive or too complex. When it comes to evening wear, simplicity is always the best way for you to go.

When you are choosing the dress that you want to wear in the evening, you need to ensure that you are able to wear it, and completely forget that you have it on. This is the best way for you to enjoy your evening without worrying about fiddling with your clothes and readjusting them.

With this guide, you will find that it is easy to dress for any time of your day, and also experience freedom when it comes to your expression of style. Once you are comfortable with what to wear and when, you will begin to realize how much you can extend yourself when it comes to your exploration of all things fashion.

Chapter 12:
Know Your Fashion Designers

There are thousands of fashion designers in the world, though only a select few have managed to remain the talk of the town. These are the designers that create trends, or style that all want to emulate. If you are working on your own style, you should look at what these designers have created and try and pick some ideas which appeal to you the most. Here are some designers that you should be familiar with: -

Coco Chanel

This is one designer that has revolutionized fashion in so many ways, including amazing clothing designs, accessories and even perfumes. Her full name was Gabrielle 'Coco' Chanel, and with her designs, the way that a woman looked in clothes was liberating. At the time that she was designing her clothing, women were still wearing clothes that restricted movement, including those that had heavy corsets.

Some of the items that she created included the Chanel Suit, which remains to this day an aspirational peace for almost every female wardrobe. She also came up with the staple concept for the little black dress, and of course, the classic Chanel 2.55 bag. Having a peace of Chanel product will be an investment due to the cost, but one that is well worth it because these pieces are classic and timeless.

Christian Dior

When you are watching fashion and style on the red carpet to get your inspiration, without a doubt you will come across a gorgeous gown that has been designed by the famed Christian Dior. This is a fashion designer who began his career designing beautiful dresses for women post war. At the time, most people were wearing clothing that can best be described as stark and lack luster.

He changed the way women felt about clothing because he brought in designs that were feminine, and so his very first collection has often been titled as 'New Look'. The result is that he created a moment that was truly iconic when it came to fashion for women, and has continued to improve on these efforts over time.

Marc Jacobs

If you are just learning about fashion and style now, this is a name you may have heard, but which you could find a challenge placing. Marc Jacobs should be your go to designer for anything that has to do with contemporary fashion today. He has been in the fashion industry for over two decades, having stepped out on the scene in the 1990s. Most of the looks that he has designed are classic and cleaned, although the inspiration for these looks has come from grunge fashion. He has his own fashion label, and he is also the creative director for leading fashion house Louis Vuitton.

Yves Saint Laurent

This is one of those brands that is distinctly recognizable, especially from the logo, and that speaks to anyone who is looking to make the most of modern style. Created by Yves Mathieu Saint Laurent, the clothes that this fashion house are most famous for are those that have clean cuts and tailoring that is often described as masculine. Designs for women that are tuxedo inspired found their start with these designs.

No matter when you see any of the designs from this fashion house, there is only one thing that really comes to mind and seems to ring true. That is the designs are based on the very best of high fashion, and modernity.

Calvin Klein

For all round fashion, you are likely to already know of the name and brand Calvin Klein. Famous for coming up with stunning fashion campaigns for underwear and perfumes,the style of clothing that you get from Calvin Klein cannot be easily found with other designers.

This is because almost all of the clothing is designed for every day wear, and is priced in such a way that the average lady can afford to purchase it. The designs and style is sophisticated, and also versatile in its nature. They include clear cuts and simple designs that appear to glide over the body of the wearer with ease.

Vivienne Westwood

Fashion designers come from all over the world, and if you are looking for an offering from Britain, then you cannot go wrong with Vivienne Westwood. This is a fashion designer that is best suited for anyone looking to achieve a daring look, or who wants to stand out from any crowd. She has successfully been designing clothing for over four decades, having started designing clothes in the 1970s.

Her inspiration is clearly from punk fashion, and she creates clothing that can best be described as pieces. Each one tells a story, stands out and is sure to be a conversation starter once you have it one.

Though she is not designing as much today as she was thirty years ago, she is still someone who is very much in the know of what is happening in fashion. When there are trends emerging, or interesting things happening with style coming up, it is highly likely that you may be referred to something that Vivienne Westwood has done to get inspired.

Giorgio Armani

Style and fashion is not only for women, as there are places that men can draw their inspiration from as well. There is no designer that has made a revolution in men's fashion as has Giorgio Armani.

When you think about the typical and coveted suit, this is the designer that will come to mind. This is due to the care that has been taken with tailoring, and ensuring that the fit of the suit is very comfortable, almost as though it is a second skin.

In fact, any man who has a high sense of fashion will lay claim to being the owner of an Armani suit, and will invest in several pieces. For fashion that stands out and makes a bold statement, this should be the staple in any clothing for men. It is also possible to get stunning Armani suits for women as well. A professional woman who wants to break through the glass ceiling should also have one of these in her wardrobe.

Valentino

Should you want to find a designer that has a distinct and unforgettable look, then consider Valentino. Valentino is known as a designer for a classic red gown. As a fashion designer, it is important to be known for one thing, and then grow form here. This makes it easy for those who want to get inspiration to identify with what the designer has to offer.

Valentino dresses are masterpieces, so much so that there are numerous ones that are features in galleries all over the world. Next time you are watching the fashion on the red carpet, keep an ear out to find out who is wearing a Valentino gown. Without a doubt, there will be someone who continues to emulate this fashion.

The next time that you want to look like a fashion icon, with a distinct and unforgettable look, ensure that you draw your inspiration from one of these amazing designers. They continue to be famous for decades because their style leaves an impact and an impression to all those who both see and wear their clothing items.

Chapter 13:
Style Around the World

If you ever get the chance to travel, you will find that people dress very differently in the various countries. Fashion means different things to different people, so when you are defining your style, you could pick some tips from other countries. Here are some style tips that may amaze you.

The Mini-Skirt

This is a fashion item that originated in the UK all the way back in the 1950s. There was actually a lady who was called Mary Quant who was responsible for making skirts so short and the word mini has nothing to do with the actual length of the skirt – at least not when it was being conceptualized. It was called a mini after the designer'sfavorite car which was the Mini Cooper.

The Kaftan

In almost all the countries of Africa, you can find women wearing a loose robe with a bold design and wide sleeves. Men have their own version which appears as though it is a robe billowing around them. This is known as the kaftan, and it is an excellent peace that will typically keep one warm when it is cold and cool when it is hot. It allows for free movement, including running, bending and moving at speed. If you are looking for inspiration from this African fashion, you can think about the design, or the print of the material.

The Kimono

Travel all the way to Asia, and specifically Japan, and you will find that women love to wear the comfortable and glamorous Kimono. If you are coming from a country where to look sexy you need to wear something short and tight, you may be surprised to discover that you can look equally sexy in an outfit that is long and straight cut. The only definition in this outfit comes from a belt that is worn around the waist.

Kimonos are available in a range of colors, although most of them tend to have reds, pinks and purples within them. They are mean to indicate love and class. Today, they have a range of embellishments including furs and jewels to stay in line with other fashions from around the world.

Pashmina

In certain Asian countries like Pakistan, where the women tend to be primarily Islamic, you will find that there are a range of pashminas available, and that most of them are made from silk. These come in numerous colors and designs and they are relatively cheap to purchase. This is great because it means that you can have a large number of them available to you. You can use these as a versatile scarf to wear on your head or on your clothing, or simply tie them on to a handbag when you need to find a way to introduce a burst of color to your outfit in the most effortless way possible.

Denim

You may be surprised to discover that denim originally came from France rather than from the United States where it has become most famous. It was Levi Strauss that led to the transformation of this material as hen used it to make the iconic jeans which almost everyone from around the world wears.

Aviator Sunglasses

These have been made famous in the United States after they have been designed for wear pilots all the way back in the 1930s. It is getting close to one century that they have been available, and now more and more people have made a pair of aviator glasses a staple in their wardrobes.

The Sari

When you see an elegant Indian lady in her traditional dress, it is highly likely that she is wearing a Sari. This is not only for women in India, but is also worn by women in Bangladesh as well as Pakistan, Malaysia and other Asian countries. No matter what shape or size a woman is, you will find that she can look absolutely amazing in a sari.

A sari is basically a long piece of material that is wrapped around the body and worn as a skirt. The end of it is slung over the shoulder as you would with a scarf. On the top, the woman wears a short top which is similar to a crop top, with a color that matches some part of the sari. The midriff is typically left bare which makes this the ideal outfit to wear when you are in a place which is hot.

There are numerous ways that you can get inspiration from around the world, or even choose to wear some of the fashions that have stood the test of time. As you continue to develop your style and your wardrobe, you will find it easier to include these items so that they join your staples and it becomes easier for you to dress.

Conclusion

You have reached the conclusion of this book, yet for your fashion journey, you are still at the starting point. Now, you have learned some essentials that will make fashion easy for you, while also helping to elevate your style. To begin with, you now know what it takes to create a basic outfit, and how you start with a base layer, and then add on more clothes and accessories until you complete your final look.

You have also learned how you can go about developing your personal style. Even though you started this book without being chic, you should have realized that this does not mean you cannot attain chic. Neither are you required to change everything about the way you dress. All that is needed it to take the right steps to express yourself, by adding interesting accessories and ensuring your clothes are well pressed. You can add elements of chic taste to any type of dress code.

The mystery of accessories has departed as you now know how you can make accessories work for any outfit you are wearing. With accessories, you can take an outfit that was drab, and instantly transform it into one that is fab.

Finally, you have an idea of some essential items that you should have in your wardrobe if you want to be chic, and how the only way that you can look your best is by embracing your body shape and dressing it up appropriately. Take your style journey into your own hands and practice everything that this book has. You will not regret it.

Fashion

Chic Style and Fashionable Outfits Guide

The 75 Most Chic & Trendy Fashion Tips to Never Leave the House Less than Amazing

Contents

Introduction

Every time you get ready to leave your home, you are likely to do something that is fairly predictable, and that is to stop and look at yourself in the mirror. This is because you want to make sure that the elements you have put together to create an outfit look amazing, and that you will also feel amazing one you are out in the world. When you are not happy about what your look like, you are possibly going to spend the entire time that you are out obsessing about whatever is not working in your overall outfit.

This does not need to be the case, as all that is necessary to help you look chic and fashionable is some tried and tested tips that have stood the test of time. In this book, you will find all the tips that you need to guarantee that you love the way you look every time you leave your home.

First, you shall discover how you can make the most of colorful pieces in your wardrobe, rather than shying away from them. You will also discover the different places that you can look for your fashion inspiration, so that you create stunning and chic looks that you love. Discover the best way that you can wear different textures as you make a statement, and how choosing beautiful accessories is an excellent way to complete any look.

If you have always wondered how you can complete an overall chic look for the last dose of confidence, steps on creating a perfect make-up look with flawless hair are also included in this book. For the only tips that you will ever need as a budding fashionista, read on!!

Chapter 1:
15 Tips on Color to Help You Glow

Dressing in colorful clothes can be intimidating, as you can get it right and look fabulous or get it wrong and look terrible. For this reason, many people tend to shy away from color in their wardrobes, opting instead to wear clothes which are neutral. It is possible that you know of someone (or it could even be you) who has a wardrobe that seems to be entirely made of black or white items. This is great for functionality, but does not do much if you are trying to be fashionable.

If you want to leave the house looking fashionable, you must inject some color into your wardrobe, and do so in such a way that you appear to be glowing from the confidence that you look your best. Here are some fabulous tips that can help you achieve that.

1. Bright Colors and Neutrals

If you are just starting out with color, then you will want to start with subtlety. The best way would be to get some neutral clothing, such as a crisp button down white shirt, and then pair this up with something that is bold and colorful, such as a knee length pencil skirt. Choose a color that is not too bright as this will help you to successfully ease into color, and feel more comfortable with what you have on.

2. Find out Which Colors Flatter You

To feel great, you must find out which colors flatter you, matching with the tone of your skin, and the colors of your hair and eyes. Normally, you will need to choose between pale colors and deep colors. To figure out which works best for you, take two pieces of your clothing, one dark and one light. Hold each piece up against you face. The tone that makes you look all lit up, and brightens your eyes and hair, is the right tone for you.

3. Prints and Monochromes

When you choose to wear a colorful print, ensure that only one item in your wardrobe has this print. For example, it could be part of your base layer, or an accessory. Rather than pairing up a range of prints and designs, pick one color from that print and every other element of your outfit should be made up of that color. If you have a bright and colorful dress with purple, yellow and blue in it, you can choose to wear a purple jacket **with** a matching bad and shoes.

4. Use Denim

If you have a very bright color making up part of your outfit, you can easily tone it down by adding some denim to the outfit. The best denim to wear for this effect should be blue, black, white or beige. With this, you will also be able to add a range of accessories, which may include subtle prints and other bright colors. Denim helps a colorful outfit look less loud.

5. Learn to Accessorize

You can add a pop of color to any outfit by building on your accessories. An excellent way to get started with this is to incorporate a bright pair of sunglasses into your outfit. To ensure that they reflect your chic style, use this accessory to follow a trend.

Accessories include jewelry, scarves, bags, and shoes – basically anything that you add to your outfit that is outside of your basic layer of clothing.

6. Pick out a Bright Bag

Whether you are wearing a monochrome outfit, or already have a little color in your outfit, you can bring out your chic style with a bright and colorful bag. Make sure that the bag is a simple design so that it looks chic rather than overwhelming or tacky. When choosing a bright bag, consider what the rest of your wardrobe looks like. There is likely to be certain tones that you like to wear. If most of your clothes tend to be brown, beige and orange or similar warm tones, you can go for a bright lemon yellow bag. However, if you have darker colors like purples, blues and grays, you can select a bag that is bright cobalt blue for a thrilling effect. This will enable you to match your bag with a myriad of items, drawing you away from a black bag that matches everything.

7. Use Neutral Colors

When you want to wear a bright color, you do not want to overwhelm your entire outfit with it. For that reason, you should incorporate some neutral colors to help to balance out the boldness. Some brilliant neutral colors to consider are khaki, navy and gray. Black and white have bene the ideal for decades, but these other neutral colors add some surprise as well as chic which can help to transform your entire outfit.

8. Pick Out Bright Shoes

You can use a pair of bright shoes to bring an outfit together, or to add character to something that would have otherwise been a boring outfit. A pair of bright pink heels will make jeans and a shirt look chic and daring, and if you wear some red heels with a little black dress you add an extra element of sexy to your wardrobe. Whether you choose to wear a pair of bright flats or stunning heels, you will find that adding a pop of color to your feet can completely transform a look, going from drab all the way to fab in seconds.

9. Try a Colorful Dress

If you are not sure about how you can match certain colors together, then you should opt to wear a dress that is colorful, saving you from trying to match up separates. Once you have this dress on, you can try and even out your favorite tones or colors in the dress by using accessories. These would include you toning down the color by coordinating your bag and shoes in a neutral color, or by picking out your favorite color in your dress and using that to create matching accessories. When you are dressed in color, you should not be too afraid of mismatching, rather, you should look for smart contrasts.

10. The Signature Accessory

Stepping out of the house in a monochrome outfit could be an indication that you have chic taste, but to add an element of style to this you need to use the right accessories. This is when a signature accessory comes in, a statement piece that you can use to add to your overall look to create something striking. A bright piece of colorful jewelry should do the trick. You could wear a pair of expressive chandelier earrings, or you could opt for a cocktail ring that has a large stone. This will incorporate color into what may have been a dull outfit.

11. Color your Hair

When wearing color, you do not need to restrict its use to your clothing. Should you follow celebrity fashion, you will notice that there are a number of people who have turned their hair into the perfect colorful accessory. Rather than going for a full dye job that is permanent, you can opt for some temporary extensions or a wig to add an element of color to any outfit that you are wearing. It is different and expressive, and choosing the right tone can help you look unbelievably chic.

12. Choose a Full Outfit

Should you choose to wear a color that you know will be difficult to match up, then it would be better to wear it as a full ensemble so that you do not have to worry about looking for matching tops or bottoms. If this is a case, go for a dress or a jumpsuit in one bold color. You can then add accessories to elevate the chic factor. Almost all colors look great with some gold accessories, so choose these to create a timeless look.

13. Different Shades of the Same Color

To wear your favorite color, you can choose a head to toe look that has different shades. This means that the top part could be a lighter shade and tone than the bottom of your outfit, and the same applies to any shoes and additional accessories you include. You can also trust that using this strategy will help you create a look that is cohesive.

14. Try Color Blocking

The best way to make a bold fashion statement though color is by color blocking. This entails you wearing different bold colors on each element of your outfit. The colors should have some contrast so that they are each able to stand out easily. You could wear a bright orange top, with a violet colored skirt and a pair of golden shoes. Although these colors are quite different, when combined into one outfit they end up creating a great look.

15. Remember your Face

A great way for you to wear color so that you glow is by incorporating into your make-up. When dressing in color, choose bright lipsticks and eye shadows that match with what you have on. When done well, bright make-up can polish off a look, helping you appear well put together and stylish. Remember that you need to have balance in your face as well. If you have a bold look, go for neutral eyes, and with powerful eye makeup, you should tone down the rest of the face.

Chapter 2:
15 Places to Find your Fashion Inspiration

As you work on creating outfits that will help you look great every time you want to leave your home, you may need to find some inspiration to help you get it right. Once you have this inspiration, you need to use it by applying what you have learned into putting together excellent outfits.

It is great to dress up in emerging trends, though you may find that what you look like in the end differs from what you picture in your mind. Rather than simply following the crowd, you can use what is available as inspiration.

To begin with, look around you and decide what you actually like. Keep a record of this by writing it down or taking pictures so that you can refer to it when you are looking to purchase some clothes. From your inspiration, it becomes possible to re-invent yourself and end up with a great look.

When looking for inspiration, the advancement of technology has played a big part since you can just source your outfit ideas online, download videos of runways, edit photos so that you can picture yourself in an outfit without having to put it on or follow the now famous fashion blogs. Fashion inspiration can be drawn from different sources with some fashion powerhouses citing art as one of the key pillars of fashion since it involves a lot of creativity. Linking art to fashion means that for creativity to translate to results, one must have an artistic mind. Here are fifteen places that you can look for inspiration:

1. Fashion Expos

Great minds in fashion will occasionally come together at a fashion expo so that they can express and share their latest contributions to the fashion world. At these expos, there are tons of inspirational pieces to explore and get really great ideas from. Here you can even get a chance to interact with the biggest names in fashion and even get a minute or two up-close and personal with your favorite designer. Fashion expos burst with a lot of creative minds and cutting edge pieces that can offer more than inspiration. When you are looking for ideas on how to choose excellent wardrobe staples or show stopping pieces, you will find what you need at an expo.

2. All Types of Art

Art is an excellent place to get inspiration from fashion, and art could even embody the creativity of someone outside yourself. The average fashion designer will find their inspiration from appreciating the art and care that another designer will use when creating their own pieces.

There is also conventional art, where one looks at how an artist uses colors and shapes on canvas. This can also help you decide what textures you can try with your clothes, or how to add an interesting twist to your wardrobe items. Look around you and review how color and design is being celebrated and expressed. This will help you get the inspiration that you need to redefine your own clothing.

3. The World Wide Web

The internet is a great place to get fashion inspiration, as there are so many different places that you can search.

Almost all fashion magazines have an online edition that you can go through to see what the latest in fashion is. To get what you need, you can use a search engine to help you find the best fashion blogs or visit the websites of your favorite designers to see what their latest creations are.

4. Movies

When you see someone dressed in 'Old Hollywood' style, you immediately recognize what they are wearing, and the elements that express this style to perfection. You can also get inspiration for fashion from movies, especially by observing the style that different characters are able to embody. Movies also help to portray certain trends and you will be able to identify how one should dress depending on their age or occupation. If you like the way a specific character is dressed, you can break down their outfit to figure out how the different elements come together to create a cohesive look.

5. Fashion Blogs

Most people are not comfortable with simply taking the word of a designer that what they have created is the next great fashion item. Instead, they prefer the opinions of real people who have to wear the clothing, and that is why fashion blogs have picked up in popularity. There are usually created by upcoming fashionistas who have a knack for putting clothes together beautifully. When looking for inspiration, you can look at these blogs and find that you identify with the person who owns and manages the blog. Their fashion sense then becomes relatable and can inspire you in various ways. Once you have identified a blog or a blogger that you can really draw inspiration from, you can even start your own blog to help inspire other people with what you have learned.

6. Fashion Magazines

Fashion magazines like Vogue continue to have a firm standing in the fashion world, especially if you are looking to find out what the latest looks and fashions trends are. These are worth keeping for inspiration, as more often than not, they feature fashion items which are timeless in their nature.

When it comes to knowing everything to do with fashion, these magazines are written and edited by seasoned award winning editors and they have accumulated numerous accolades over the years. Fashion magazines have photos that have been taken by professional photographers and these photos can provide inspiration especially if you cut them and try and match with whatever is in your wardrobe.

You can also get inspiration by sharing your views in the opinion section of the magazine. You will get responses and opinions from others in the world of fashion and this can help you shape the way you want to dress. Constant contributions can earn you a viable spot in the magazine. From here, you can interact with the editors or even the models for inspiring ideas!

7. Television Shows

TV shows are just like movies but the difference is that the newer the show, the fresher the trends. People watch new shows to get a glimpse of what is fresh and trendy and a huge percentage of most TV shows today are based on fashion.

TV shows are great places to find inspiration, as each character is well thought out and there is a huge team of stylists that work towards ensuring that the fashion stays true to the character. When you are looking for inspiration for timeless pieces, you should watch shows which are old school as they are able to help you establish a bridge or link to the new and fluctuating trends.

8. Fashion Shows and Runways

When you are looking to get inspiration from the latest and greatest, then you need to check out fashion shows and runways. It is on these platforms that the trends in fashion will emerge. If you are unable to attend a fashion show, then all you need to do is look for it online and you will be able to find the best videos and pictures that accentuate the key pieces from the shoes. You can also visit the sites of fashion powerhouses, as they update their looks regularly.

9. Music

You can use music for fashion inspiration in a range of ways. To begin with, the genre of music has an effect on the way that artists dress. This is such that some dressing styles are compared to music, such as bohemian looks and rocker chic. Musical artists tend to also use clothing as a creating outlet to set the mood for their own working environment.

In addition to the music artists themselves, going to a musical concert where there are huge crowds is a great way to get inspiration from fashionista fans. With artists, there are those who have successfully become ambassadors for fashion houses and your favorite artist can then inspire your wardrobe.

10. Nature

Fashion inspiration began with the elements where the earliest people used leaves to create pieces that covered up their bodies. All colors come from nature, consider the flowers in the environment. To get inspiration, you should visit parks, exotic cruises, safaris and the like. These can help you develop fresh ideas that you can use to incorporate into your clothing.

11. Daily Life

Life is a good teacher and in this case, a good inspiration. Personal experiences can bring out fresh and unique ideas that can deeply inspire you. Take the time to observe what is happening all around you, and you will find that there are events and people who inspire your sense of fashion. This is excellent as often you also have to look within yourself to establish what works for you and inspires you.

12. Large Events

Events that are fashion focused are great places for you to seek for and find fashion inspiration. Consider events where there is a large red carpet and people are wearing the very latest that fashion has to offer. These could be big events like the Academy awards, the Grammys and the Emmys. Here, designers showcase their most stunning offerings by dressing up the celebrities that are in attendance, which helps to make distinct style statements.

13. Press and Posters

Most promotions are placed on posters and billboards. In these, there will be photographs of people who are fashionable dressed. Since care is taken to properly represent a product, event or whatever the model is working towards, you can trust that the outfit worn has been put together with thought. This makes press and posters viable for seeking fashion inspiration.

14. Mail Catalogues

Although this is a more traditional method of finding inspiration, it is still a great and tangible way to pique your fashion senses. This is because you can easily cut out pieces from a catalogue to create an album that embodies the different styles that you would like to try. You will find this a great source of inspiration as it enables you to look outside the box on what is being offered.

15. Books

Books are full of inspirational fashion ideas if you take the time to go through them in detail. Consider a historical romance that describes the way that women dressed centuries ago. You may find that you want to try out brocade fabrics or create some gloves made from delicate lace once you have completed reading one of these books. With books, you get your creative juices going, and you can find the elements that you need to put together so that you end up with a fabulous final look.

Chapter 3:
12 Timeless Pieces every Wardrobe Should Have

When it comes to planning a wardrobe and its essentials, you need to focus on getting pieces which are timeless. Fashion is ever changing, as fads and trends come and go. Although fashion is dynamic, there are aspects which always remain, even if they may vary slightly due to the times. There are basic foundations that a wardrobe requires. These are the 'building blocks' to that wardrobe, the things that are timeless and will never go out of style. This section sheds light on the items that are chic and stylish, which should be present in every closet.

1. Pencil Skirt

This is a staple item that forms the base of many outfits which are worn to the workplace. The good news about having a pencil skirt is the fact that it is highly versatile and can be worn outside the office as well. A pencil skirt will go well with a fancy top or shirt, so that you can transform it into part of an evening outfit with ease. Try and have a pencil skirt that is in a neutral color as this will ensure that it matches with a wide array of items. This is a skirt that should stop just above the knee and follow your body smoothly rather than cling on to you.

2. Blue Jeans

This is one of those fashion items that can make your body look amazing. The right style of blue jean will highlight the best parts of your body, showing off the length of your legs or clinging to your curves. In addition, this is an item that can be easily dressed up or dressed down meaning that you can wear it at any time of day or night. When dressing up for a casual day at the office, you can wear a white buttoned shirt with your blue jeans. For a quick errand, you can put on a pair of blue jeans with a t-shirt and sneakers, or for a night out on the town, pair your blue jeans with a tailored blazer and a pair of high heels.

3. The Tailored Blazer

There are few items that can instantly class you up like a well-fitting tailored blazer. This is an item that you can easily combine with a whole host of other items, including skirts and trousers as well as all types of dresses. When made from the right material and featuring clean lines and a nice shape, this is an item that will always leave you looking polished. You can modernize the basic blazer with a range of accessories.

4. The LBD (Little Black Dress)

Enter into any fashion circle and you will hear loud whispers of the classic LBD which is often called the closet cliché. It is perhaps the most coveted item in any closet. When you have selected the right LBD you will be able to wear it for almost all occasions including social functions, cocktail parties, church, a date and more. This is one piece that you are guaranteed will never go out of style. The key to getting this item right is to find an LBD that works for your body.

These dresses are available in every shape and size, so if you are curvy, there is no need to get anxious. Simple search for an LBD that is the fit and flare style. This is the only *dress that can be worn on all occasions without eyebrows being raised, or feeling as though you are out of place.

5. Ballerina Flats

High heels are amazing as they always make on look tall and sexy as they elongate the legs. They are also not the most comfortable of footwear, and after extensive periods of wearing, all you want to do is take them off so that you can give your feet some much needed relief. This is when you need to have a classic pair of ballerina flats. These flats do not need to be plain and simple so that they match everything. Find a color or a print that you like which is chic and appealing. You can also choose ballerina flats that have a little embellishment on them. They can be worn will all types of clothing, including a pair of trousers when you are going to the office, or a floaty sundress when going for a picnic over the weekend.

6. Fitted Black Trousers

Just like the little black dress, this is also a closet cliché. What's amazing about a pair of fitted black trousers is that they are an all-rounder and are suitable for wear on all occasions and at any time of year. If you are going on a weekend getaway, this item can easily be matched up with an array of tops and accessories. When on a shopping spree, a pair fitted black trousers will help you gauge how other items look on your body and match up, and when you want to go out with friends, add some heels and a glittery top and you will look amazing. To ensure that this wardrobe item looks chic, you need to have the right material that looks great when it is well pressed. You should also try and get a pair of fitted black trousers that is perfectly tailored and which stops at the ankle, a position where it will not be too long or too short.

7. Boots

There are so many different types of boots that you can choose from. There are knee high boots which are perfect for wearing in the cold weather, then you also have thigh high boots which are deliciously sexy. However, the type of boots that stand the test of time are ankle boots, and this is what you need to have in your wardrobe. They are able to match with all types of clothing, including skirts and dresses, jeans and more. Even when styles and trends come and go in fashion, these will always remain relevant. They should be made from leather or suede, and you can wear them to almost all occasions.

8. Handbag

This is an item that you will always have with you, as there are things that you must carry around when you leave the house. Rather than just throwing your essentials into any old bag, you should make sure that you have a handbag that is timeless and looks amazing. To get it right, you need to have a bag that is medium sized. This will stand the test of time. You should look for one that has adjustable straps, so that you can carry it as a handbag with short straps, or for variation, you can elongate the straps and wear it as a cross body bag. A great color for your standard handbag is black, as it will match with anything that you put on without overwhelming your outfit. Get a bag that is not branded with many embellishments. The best material for your handbag is leather and the ideal shape is something that is boxy.

9. White Sneakers

You will always look well put together and organized with a pair of crisp and clean white sneakers on your feet. These are ideal for going on an evening walk, or pairing with a pair of shorts when going to the shops. They should not be too sporty, as you are not looking for an athletic shoe. They should be simple, with a rubber sole, and laces in the front. When you find a stylish and fashionable pair, you can be sure that they will stand the test of time.

10. White T-Shirt, White Button Down Shirt and White Tank Tops

When it comes to items that you need to cover your upper body, you cannot go wrong with a classic white piece. These are especially chic as they can easily be accessorized and always make one look neat and polished.

A whit button down shirt is ideal for all occasions and can be worn underneath blazers, sweaters and trench coats. This is an item that can make you look professional when paired with items that you would wear to the office. Ensure that it is well pressed and has clean lines for the greatest fashion effect.

In all weather, you can always wear a white tank top underneath your clothes. This is an item that is able to match with anything that you put on, and also looks great underneath a shirt with open buttons or tucked into a maxi skirt.

You can use a white t-shirt for all occasions as well, especially when you are putting together a chic casual outfit. It is great for all occasions and looks amazing when it is paired up with jeans.

11. Silk Scarf

This is a delicate item that will make you look chic from the moment that you put it on. You must have a brightly colored silk staff in your wardrobe. It can have a print on it or not, either way, you will find that you can match it up with an array of items. This is the wardrobe piece that will add life to anything that you wear, no matter how plain or monochromatic that it may be. Be careful about matching a printed scarf with printed clothes. You may be doing too much and end up looking clownish. It is better for a printed scarf to be matched to something plain, and for a plain scarf to dress down a bold print.

12. Sunglasses/Glasses

This is the easiest accessory to put on to instantly change the way that an outfit looks. You can make an outfit look chic with this versatile accessory. As a wardrobe staple, you must invest in a great pair of sunglasses, preferably with a black frame that can easily match any items in your wardrobe. They can make a dress or a suit look chic, adding an element of glamour to your wardrobe, or even making you look professional.

When you are out of the weekends, or spending some time with friends, a good pair of sunglasses can help polish off your jeans and t-shirt look.

All of these timeless pieces should form the foundation of your wardrobe and are the perfect items to put together when you are looking at building your closet. With them, you can create an array of looks by combining various accessories. You can look chic and fancy for any occasion, and with accessories, you will be able to dress them up to follow the ever fluctuating fashion trends. When you have all the above items, learn how you can mix and match them so that you look classy.

There is one thing that you can count on when considering these items, and that is the fact they will never go out of style. You do not need to be a fashionista to own or dress in any of these items. Even with little or no idea of how to put clothes together, putting on these timeless pieces will ensure that you always look great, whether you need something that is casual or are dressing up for a professional function.

Chapter 4:
10 Ways to Treasure Texture

Now that you are in the world of fashion, you will have realized something interesting about clothes and fabrics. They are made from a range of different materials, and for that reason, they have different looks and feels. When you decide that you want to wear textures, you may find that you need to incorporate different patterns and styles together as well so that you create an overall cohesive look. Here are ten ways that you can treasure texture for great results.

1. Understand your Casual Textures

There are certain textures that are ideal for casual wear, and these will quite often go well with a pair of jeans. You can incorporate these textures into different accompanying items and accessories when creating your outfit. The first of these is suede. This is a material that you will usually find on shoes or jackets, though it is also used to make accessories like handbags and chokers. It feels soft and expensive to the touch. Then there is leather, which can be smooth and polished, giving a shiny look, or you can find it in a matte style.

Leather was traditionally used for making shoes and handbags, but now, you can class up your outfit with a timeless leather jacket or leather leggings that look like liquid against your skin. Cotton is the material that is often used in making t-shirts, and it has a soft and familiar feeling texture. Tweed looks and feels a little rough, and it features what appears to be many tiny little squares. This is a heavier texture that is ideal on jackets or full suits. When you want to create a casual outfit, you can layer your clothing to incorporate these textures.

2. Understand your Glamour Textures

When putting together a glamourous outfit for evening wear, you need to choose textures which are luxurious and chic. You cannot go wrong with anything that is made from silk. Silk is smooth to the touch and has a little bit of shine to it. It is a material that looks expensive, and indeed it is. When you wear a scarf that is made of silk, then you will be linked with a sense of chic style. If your entire outfit is made from silk, in addition to looking stylish, you will also appear to be delicate.

Satin is another shiny material that looks highly luxurious. It is often used in creating evening dresses that are meant to be show stoppers. It is able to cling to one's curves and highlight the body's best feature, and that is why so many women opt to wear satin when they want to feel fantastic. It is a little heavier than silk. Then there is chiffon which is light, flowy and airy, making one appear as if the clothes that they have on were effortless. It is ideal for wearing to all occasions, especially celebrations like wedding. When you wear anything made from chiffon, you will feel free and confident.

To add a sense of romanced to your clothing, you can select textures like lace, velvet or organza. Lace is all about attention to detail, where intricate designs are placed against the skin such that they are well highlighted and look brilliant. Velvet is soft and luxurious, and associated with anything to do with wealth. Organza also has a fabulous sheen to it that makes it the ideal material and texture for chic evening wear.

What is great about these textures is they can easily be worn together and matched up with a host of brilliant accessories.

3. Keep to the Same Color and Theme

Consider that you want to incorporate the soft and silky texture of a scarf, with the rough to the touch texture of a pair of jeans. This will help you achieve a chic look that communicates that you are feminine, but should not be messed with either. The best way to pull this off so that your look appears seamless is by ensuring you wear items which are the same color. This is more easily done when you have a pattern. For example, you may have a scarf that is pink with white polka dots. You can match this up with a white pair of jeans and you will look stunning. This will help you to make a great fashion statement.

4. Work with Knitwear

There are many variations of knit wear, and these are an excellent way for you to include texture in your wardrobe. Whether you are wearing a chunky knit sweater, or you have a fine knit woolen top on, you can create a stunning outfit by pairing this with a plain linen pencil skirt. This adds elegance to the pairing, helping you to accentuate your figure even if your knit outfit is not body hugging. Knitwear is a highly versatile yet effective way that you can include texture in your outfits. If you look properly, you will find that you can wear different types of knitwear in all seasons, so you do not need to believe that this type of clothing is only restricted to the cold season.

5. Mix Up your Thick and Light Textures

You can achieve a brilliant overall look by mixing up your textures, choosing to pair thick and light textures in one outfit. This creates a fabulous contrast that helps every element of your outfit stand out. You can wear a top that is made from lace with a knitwear skirt and top this up with a leather jacket. With this combination you add some romanticism to a tough look. You could also wear a plain pair of black tights and top this with a leather fringe bag and leather jacket. This accentuates the texture and appearance of the fringe, but the plain black tights help to ensure that the other elements are not too overwhelming.

6. Create Beautiful Contrasts

When you are looking to create some crossover styles, you can combine casual textures with glamour textures for a fantastic result. Consider putting an outfit together that has suede in the shoes and jacket, chiffon for the skirt and a cotton shirt. This will help you look feminine and romantic, but also give you an edge in your overall look.

If you want to create a look that has an edge to it, you can wear a leather jacket that features some smooth studs with a long linen skirt. You will also appear to be chic and stylish, while also being able to express a more distinct personal style.

7. Choose Something Opulent

Most of the textures so far have been relatively subtle and able to blend in easily with the basic outfit. If you are really looking to make a strong statement, you could choose to do so by wearing a texture that is highly opulent. This would include something like a feather boa or a large faux fur jacket. When you wear items of this nature, they become statement pieces and carry the rest of the outfit. They go best with clothes which are monochromatic, and which they are able to match with in some way. This will give you that element of chic that is carried off with great confidence.

8. Go Cultural

Many cultural or traditional clothing have rich textures, and wearing these can help you use texture to make a fashion statement. Consider a beautiful plaid skirt that has a wooly texture. You can pair this skirt with leather leggings, giving your chic look some edge to it. You could also choose an Aztec inspired leather dress and pair with flat and soft suede shoes. Not only will you look like you are dressing in full cultural regalia, you will also have mixed textures beautifully.

For something more dramatic, you can look to the east. In countries like India, texture is added to an outfit through sequins and gaudy accessories that are dramatic and bright. Using materials that you can add on to your clothing, including embroidery, is an excellent way that you can embrace texture to make a fashion statement.

9. Try some Tights

When you are unsure about trying different textures in one outfit, you can begin by experimenting with tights. When wearing rough tweed, choose a pair of smooth tights with a satin finish. With a short cotton skirt, choose lace tights that add some drama. You will be amazed by how using this item for texture can transform your entire look and outfit.

10. Keep one key piece

You do not want to overwhelm your entire outfit when you are working with textures, and therefore, it is essential that you have one key piece in your entire outfit that has the texture focus. For example, this could be a pair of trousers that are brocade. Build everything around this heavy texture, and if you want to add any other items that have some texture, they should be lighter and easily mesh with the main item.

The moment you choose to treasure your texture so that you feel fabulous when you leave your home, keep in mind that different seasons require different textures. If you use this to guide your decisions, it will be much easier to incorporate the right pieces into your wardrobe.

Chapter 5:
13 Ways to Work your Jewelry and Handbags

For the most part, when you are selecting accessories that will match with your outfit, you will be looking at making the most of jewelry and handbags. There are a broad range of designs and styles that you can choose from, especially if you are working towards looking chic and fashion forward. When creating your wardrobe, you can have some timeless pieces that you wear often, but with jewelry, you have the freedom to stay on trend and have a wide variety of piece that you can choose from.

Purchasing jewelry does require you to invest thousands on each piece so that you have a collection of gold, silver and precious stones. You can have a range of cosmetic and beaded jewelry that make excellent accessories at a fraction of the cost. Here are some options worth considering.

1. The Bib Necklace

To make a chic statement, especially over monochromatic classic fashion pieces, you should wear statement bib necklace. This piece of jewelry adds much needed drama to an outfit, and will make you look stylish in an instant. You can choose a bib necklace that is gold in color, or opt for something a little more dramatic made from beads and metal. These necklaces are best for dressing up an outfit.

2. Keep it Simple and Elegant

You can use jewelry to look chic by keeping it simple and elegant. For example, you could wear stud pearl or diamond necklaces to add an element of class to your outfit. If you want to match these with a necklace, a simple string of pearls is ideal, as is a necklace that features a pendant with a small diamond. This also extends to the watch that you choose, as a no-fuss design it great as it would match with everything. If you want to add some character to your jewelry, you could try a charm bracelet.

3. The Dress Watch

Most people will wear a watch for purely functional reasons to tell the time, but if you must wear an accessory, you can make sure that it is chic and stylish so that it makes a fashion statement. The best watches are dress watches, and these often feature metallic watch bands that are in either gold or silver. Watches that have leather or plastic straps do not make the cut.

The watch that you have should fit your wrist well, so that it is not moving around too much or cutting off your circulation. For an expression of your personal style, you may select a watch that has also been embellished with crystals in a design that you like.

4. Get Some Cubic Zirconia

Even though you may not be able to afford precious and semi-precious stones, you can still get some great imitation jewelry by stocking up in some cubic Zirconia pieces. This is a stone that is known for being clear and available in a great range of colors. It looks just as great as the real thing, so when you wear it, you will feel fabulous as well.

5. Hoop Earrings

When you want to wear a statement necklace or some bright bracelets that extend up most of your forearm, then you need something simple and subtle to prevent yourself from looking gaudy and as if you are trying too hard. This is what hoop earrings are for. They are an excellent expression of chic style, and can be work with almost any outfit. You will find that they are available in many different sizes, but the best would have diameter of one to two inches.

6. Chandelier Earrings

As you prepare for a night out, you can add a lot of glamour to your outfit with some dangly chandelier earrings. The best should be in gold and silver, and they can be embellished with colorful stones. These are a statement piece for jewelry and therefore when you wear them, you should not try to add in too many other elements.

7. Cocktail ring

If you need a piece of jewelry that is sure to be a conversation starter, then you should have a cocktail ring in your jewelry set. This will always make you look fashion forward and chic. A cocktail ring can be quite eye catching, as it requires a large oversized stone to make a statement. Match the stone to the color that you are wearing, or, if you want to make a statement that is dramatic, opt for a ring that has dark, rich colors. This is also an unobtrusive addition to any outfit.

In addition to jewelry, you can elevate your outfit by choosing a fantastic handbag. The thing with handbags is there are so many styles to choose from, once you start making purchases, you will likely continue to build up your collection. Your bag needs to be large enough to carry your most important items, including your keys, make-up, cellphone and wallet. However, it should be more than a practical addition to your wardrobe. It needs to make a statement as well. Here are some styles you are sure to love: -

8. The Hobo Handbag

When you need a style that is casual and relaxed, but is able to add the element of chic to any outfit that you put on, then the best option you can have is the hobo handbag. This is a bag that does not have rigid lines and structures. It is more rounded in nature, and that is the reason that it appears to be more casual. A leather hobo handbag is excellent because it will match with almost everything and is also easy to clean and maintain.

9. The Clutch Purse

Going out for the evening requires you to add elements to your look that add sophistication and grace, and nothing accomplishes that quite as well as the clutch purse. These bags are available in a range of sizes, so that you can fit all your essentials into the bag. Their typically rectangular in shape and appear boxy, though it is possible to find variations that feature rounded edges for a much softer look.

10. The Tote Bag

Every wardrobe needs to have a standard tote bag for everyday use. These are available in various sizes, and in them, you can easily carry all of your daily essentials. These bags are made to be much stronger and longer lasting than the typical bag, which is why they are ideal for heavy use. Choose one that is in a neutral color like brown or black, and then for matching with specific outfits, get as many colors as you can.

Conclusion

You are now ready to step out into the world and express yourself as a well put together and chic fashionista. The 75 tips that you have read are just what you need to ensure you are able to stay on trend and look perfect, every single time that you leave your home.

From these tips, you have learned some essential things to note about fashion, right from the moment that you are making the decision to wear a certain outfit, to the time when you put the finishing touches to your look.

You know what it takes to create the base of your wardrobe, which is the foundation of any outfits that you are looking to create. When you have a good base, you have the freedom to mix and match different elements so that you achieve a stunning final piece. You now understand why the best fashionistas always have a fitting pair of jeans, crisp white shirt and tailored blazer.

To finish off an outfit, you now know what you need to do to pick a great handbag that will complement the style of what you are wearing, and also your body shape and size. Through all the lessons and tips that have been highlighted in this book, there is one that stands out and that is to be yourself. Use these tips to accentuate your own natural style so that you always leave the house both looking and feeling amazing.